Published by Draft2Digital,United States.

support@draft2digital.com

https://www.draft2digital.com/

Longing for Light under the Abyss

By

Creator of Eden

4951 Alavista Dr
Orlando, FL, 32837
creatorofeden10@gmail.com

Table of Content

Section I: Journeying through the Living

1. Piece of the Light   5
2. Last Breath   7
3. Christmas: Child of Winter   9
4. Is Truth of True Existence   11

Section II: Embracing Dust

5. Fallen from the Edge   13
6. Songs of Eden   15
7. Heart of Stone   18

Section III: Finding Grace within Darkness

8. My Valentine   20
9. Light of the Abyss   24
10. Dawn of Stillness   28

Piece of the Light

Chasing the bright green light.
Radiant upon the Crossings.
Of a heavenly sky glowing at the west.
Feet galloping on the grass.
Spreading his legs in frantic motion.
Reaching out with one arm.
To feel the embrace of angelic warmth.
Before it dissipates into the starlit background.

Autumn winds pushing back with harshness.
Refusing you the light you've been seeking.
Since you've been a babe, having been a
witness.
Of generations of people around.
From comrades to family.

Chasing the green light.

Running in many paths to feel the fire above heaven.

Desiring for it to be the salvation of their wandering souls.

For it to make their soul whole and their existence in this world assured.

Many succeed, and more fail.

Spirits of the ones whose visions were never met.

Illuminates the atmosphere from the celestial streams beyond glowing candles above.

To beneath the surface of apathetic critters and grassroots.

You are determined to not be part of those that'd fallen.

So as the green light steadily diminishes itself into the background.

You begin to rush yourself as the leaves of summer pass by you.

Earnestly going all the way to a high cliff, pushing against the immortal air with naive courage.

As you stand up there with your toes at the tip of the edge.

The green light fades and evaporates from the night sky.

Internally yearning for it to return, the feeling of failure begins to emerge.

A lost soul you've felt is the only destination as you walk the forest of life.

Then you aim yourself down and realize the deep ocean depths below.

Taking a step back with haste, you take a breath in relief.

Thinking of how many had fallen chasing the light.

Then you look down again from a safer angle and notice a glistening green light shining from the deep sea.

You marvel at the beauty of it, as it continues to shine more fiercely, more so than even from the green light itself.

Turning towards your arms, then your legs, steadily seeing the light glitter all around your body in a united creed.

As you focus upon the ocean, mainly on its light, you steadily realize that the light is a reflection of your being.

Paying attention more to the autumn leaves as they pass by, becoming more aligned with the once adversary wind as it blows your hair and letting it dance in tune.

Becoming fully aware of the presence of the green light upon yourself.

You walk away from the cliff, internally at peace, with the green light gracefully shining in a muse.

As you walk with a piece of the light.

Last Breath

Help I Cry
Death is here
No more flight
Health is queer

All self is dying
Ego, Spirit, body
Call to reclaim rising
I do, of personal country

Glory ceasing of existence
Memories withdrawing
Truly releasing all magnificence
Of centuries of pain releasing

All unto me.
Unacceptable it must
Fall I should not cross me
Unrepentant it must

My soul, immortal it was
Prestige, fame, honor
Bestow glory, goods
Merit, game, struggle

Above laws, nature and men
So I thought, based on skill alone
Beyond the punishment of lower ones then
Cold and hard, refusing to atone

Now my being is ceasing
Soul never reaches flight
Loud I cry for mercy and decreasing
Of world ever reaching naught

Praising himself for breathing
Thinking it's work of my own
Forgetting self to consider openness
Quickly, it ends with cancellation of my show
Watching is Mother Earth with stoic glance

Love, life, liberty
Disappearing inevitably
Tears, regret, confusion
Coming inevitably

Pain of the soul, spirit, mind
Last thoughts as I
Lay my Last Breath.

Christmas: Child of Winter

Lights glistening across the earth and sea
Upon all residences on soil and air
Nights and Days shines mesmerizingly
Even as brightness falls from the clouds in ease

Heaven-born snow falling onto the ground
Creating bedsheets of the purity of existence
As it covers most of the world with mourning
shroud
Revealing solemn spread surface bare skin from
aesthetics

Dying crops and harvest are static in presence

With seeds of eternities underneath the
carcasses
Lying on frosts and marvels are old breeds
paying final penance
In knowing creed letting fragilities underneath
naked in stone promises

Choirs of communities from families to friends
Giving gifts of physical artistic allure and
spiritual radiance
Fire of elation and bliss spreading unambiguous
with seeming no ends
Nesting in others the importance and memories
of needed joy of magnificence

Many use it as opportunities to return feet back
to the fields
To ensure the remembrance of our mortality
For those craving for superficial legacy that's
omnipresent and clean

New realizations may appear in able to bring
heaven within to the scene

To ensure the creation of our true immortality

Harsh and cold yet soft and moist
Winter is unforgiving yet merciful
Marsh of pale old leaves unvoiced
Sender of relentless yet beautiful

Saga of dense temporary and enduring pain
Yet immortal transcendence of rising endurance
Flora awaits as the mist of earthly tensions
remains untamed
Flesh of anything mortal dissipating for coming
of the collective enlightenment

Upon the atmosphere to the grass fields and
onto the human spirit

As children hear of legends of givers of
presents, heroism and sacrifice that persist
Amongst them as they listen with glee of loving
caregiver bringing joy with jubilant lyric
Some may also hear of one's humility of facing
personal winter to rise again as eternal spring

Winds blowing across plains and cool rivers
Carriers of the wills of Winter
Binds old wisdom with new silver
Cherishing the wills of Nature

Continuing this tradition
With its son Christmas

Is Truth of True Existence

Truth in meaning, absolute, and final.
Myth is inst in analytical presentation.
Proof plain as cornfields for the tribal.
Bliss it should bring, creating expansion.

Of intellectual and better understanding of
humanity.
Or across a version of particular sentient being's
view.
Sun's light may be rising above a crew's ship
with infinity.
Sun's light may be setting downward with
fragility in a hiker's view

One looks below from mountains embracing the beauty of the songs of life.
Another looks above at mountains accepting the futility of all breathers of life.
Songs of courage, honor, bravery, and self-sacrifice is the golden rule of earth.
Fathers and mothers uphold it as ultimate truth of and beyond this world.

Thoughts of blooming progress of ideals enter living seedlings proto-rebirthed.
Creators of new thinking, self-seeing, insistence on longevity exceed mortal lore.
Songs of intellect, liberty, equality, and self-sufficiency is the golden rule of earth.
Fathers and mothers uphold it as ultimate truth of and beyond this world.

Since breathing first breath there's a claim of the ultimate and rigorous truth.

Every Sapient desires to be the discoverer of what is true in the unpredictability of life.
Clench and seething many tribes grasp and claim of holding key to truth
Vary are successes upon perception doesn't guarantee foundations of life.

Many shall make claims of knowledge of the real truth of being.
Enforcing it some may mistake truth for ideals of experience.
Plenty shall assert their claims as universal and natural upon order of existence.
Relating the human model to the expansive nature and cosmos of one's creation.

Although nature itself as well as beyond the stars shows usual indifference.
Nature guides itself in order without question or reflection.

Master of seasons, currents, patterns with the stone-cold precision
With the cosmos expanding its magnificence in graceful determination.

Two entities paying no mind to our attempt of limiting monumental work
To our need to merge all consciousness into a collective unification
Fool's to be is no one's wish, ceasing from finding one's crutch

Eyes of one may see our species with wonder, pride, allure, and empathy.
The eyes of another may see our species with anger, regret, disgust, and apathy.
Eyes of one see that one should reach out for the suns of heaven.
The eyes of another see that one should remain in the dust of Eden.

Absoluteness of Truth of possibilities or
disillusions?
Is it dependence on facts or appeal?
Solutions of unearthing truth solutions or
hallucinations?

Is there justice not based on the trappings of the
planet?
Time limit known only on this globe?
Are there possibilities of desires beyond the
planet?
Signs of a guiding parent figure, origin of the
everlasting, is it of our core?

Is morality as known, the truth?
Is it based on limited scopes of vision?
If one feels it is true, should one act as living
proof.

If one does, shall it be of a mortal lie even as believed as truth?

Morality exists above humanity.
Myth or Fact?
Sincerity exists in one's heart within humanity.
Since limbs, first drawn.

Believability of one's wisdom as
all-encompassing.
Long journeys of us all from wandering flocks of dust.
To souring white angels across moons.
Flocks of animals we are yearning with hearts internally rust.

For the wonderment if Truth is of True Existence.

Fallen from the Edge

Below somber dark sky
With clouds covering moonlight
Stars nowhere to be seen
As if a distant memory

Feet on ledge of Bridge
Bridge calm and still
Eye's gaze down
On flowing ocean waters

Winds blowing across body
Chilling sensation on skin
Skin Hair breezing backward
Eyes vacant and void

Pocket going into hand

A black metal pistol is revealed
Arms raised. Gun in hand
Barrel placed on right side of head

Breathing remains steady
Tears fall from eyes
Releasing a smile, a first smile
Not released for millennia

As tears flow down and join the ocean
The index fingers pull the trigger
Mind is blank and black

Body flings itself downwards
It's descending down
Until it hits the water
The corpse motions along

With the ocean currents
Never to be seen or heard again

Now able to lay to rest at last

Songs of Eden

The Golden Sun always shining on you
It's the very creator of your majestic hair
A part of the always glistening beauty that's you
It's the very nature of your majestic confident
air

And in that air, under the sun, below the grass
You are an energy of such gentle grace
Mellow-like soft winds blowing the grass
Giving anything you pass by, life and flesh.

Your irksome giggling and laughing
Is the music of warmth to my freezing heart
Your amazing curiosity and intelligence
Is the melodies to my yearning heart

Fiery, fierce, and fearless as an eternal flame
Scary as hell, yet so alluring and enduring
Maybe it's a good idea to run away to not get flamed
Yet can't help but want to reach the fire, even risking pain

Yet pain is what I'm willing to embrace
If only to get to the roses underneath the thorns
That's part of a beautiful plentiful soil as you are
That I hope to be allowed to help grow it's potential

It can be seen not all is flawless in the earthly paradise
Weeds, cockroaches, and other disgusting traits of nature

Is all revealed from underneath your imperfect
being
Seeing all of these things should convince me to
leave you behind

It doesn't, all these features are within me as
they are in you
For it's not disqualifying your unique nurturing
substance of life
All it does is make you real.
A true living, breathing residence of life

Whose imperfections can be watered and settled
in due time
I'm willing to see through your weeds and
thorns
To get to the pure kind soul that's within you
Not to mask them in leaves and acorns

But to help cut them out to help create growth within you

Above the golden sun, I see birds fly like angelic beings

They fully represent your transcendent independent spirit

Flying their wings with such refinement and nobility

Above the golden sun, as you do every day under it

We all know that anything with wings can fall

Birds and even angels alike, yet if you fall

My arms will be opening, ready to catch your fall

If it comes, you fall out of your rightful place in heaven

For the garden that is you

One must be there for when you rain

And not just when your rivers are clean

For the garden that is you
I hope to be let in your soulful world
To be your spring when your heart's in winter
I hope to be let in your river of eternal grace

To be your rock when your heart's in a
hurricane
If in your everlasting eye's
Your wisdom says it shall not be me
If in your everlasting eye's

I'm unable to care for the noble soil
That is you
Then it is so
For you
That is so

If another can make you smile

Then it will warm my empty heart regardless
It'll hurt to not be your rock along the river tides
But your smile and happiness is of most
importance regardless

And so this all to you is my composition
For my eternal beautiful imperfect garden
And so this is the last line of my song
My Song for Eden.

Heart of Stone

Hoodie covering face
Solemn and Stoic
Hands-on pockets
Warm and Rested

Feet walking on sidewalk
Steady and Rigid
Passing by others
Steady yet energetic

Sun above present
Shining light on everyone
Yet never touching you
Nor your heart

Weather is warm
Yet you feel cold
Sky is blue
Yet you feel black

As a void
Everyone passing by
Smiling, laughing, joyful
As you continue strolling
Frowning, moping, mournful

Soul closed, guarded, gated
People are open, expressive, free
Street's lively, animated vibrant
Eyes dead, empty, barren

Summer is here for everyone
Winter is eternal for you
Grace is dead
Embrace is Myth

Walking down street
Heart of Stone

My Valentine

Sitting on glass table
Staring at reflection
Rain dripping from eyes
Pain rising from solitude

I'm the only presence
In an empty house
I'm the only presence
In empty life
My heart beats slow
For love in this day
Every day, I hope

I breathe in. I breathe out
Tension dissipates within
Turning and looking
Hoping for wondrous love

To come.

Though never did
Never will

Swimming waves
Of hurt and pain
Flowing and splashing
In between open sinkhole
Within my Being

Intense is my desire
For love and affection
That I so want
Yet never get

Mind wanders
I morph into past self
As the waves within

Intensified in magnitude

I'm a little child

Crying for mommy and daddy
For hugs, kisses, touches
Stop crying. Get over it.
Mommy and daddy proclaim

So I hope for love among lovers
For hugs, kisses, touches
Stop being needy
So I hope for love among
Silence. My only love
I see television and reality
Flowers, roses, kissing
Laughing, teasing, loving

Everywhere, except this table
Love, compassion, affection

My heart aches for
Never given by any family
Nor any women

A woman appears
As if ghost
Caresses my hair
Giggles with me

We kiss, I close eye's
I open it, she's gone
For she never existed
Except as brief comfort

Sinkhole widens more
Waves clash around
From within my soul
That aches on this day

Getting up, getting myself cake

Sitting back down, chewing up
Eating it, enjoying it, content
All aching forgotten, briefly

I see red rose in vase
Facing me in gentle bliss
Don't mind if I do
I take off vase

And place gently

In front of me
As gift to myself
One I deserve
Even from myself

Contentment in loneliness
Looking in mirror
Tears dry and faded
I smile at myself

Sinkhole within closing
Waves steadily flow back
Sweet taste in mouth
I realize my truth

No one will ever love me
Therefore I must love myself
Contentment in Solitude
Must be a commitment

Staring down at glass table
Eyes on reflection
I nod my head
Seeing my lover

I'll always be committed
To you
My love
My valentine.

Light in the Abyss

My Lord, for today, is a New Year
It's 2024, a new beginning.
As promised by the world
As stated by you, the Most High.

While trials and tribulations abound
Fields of fruits and gold
Would surpass all suffering
At least in naive mind

For the Sun is up
Promising new beginnings
Yet, I suffer still
Pain and emptiness maintain

It was naivety that caused the heart
To dream of a new beginning
Of career springboards

New beginnings
Doesn't must mean
That a greater Good
In life is coming near

It could mean the exact opposite
The Lord said to me
This is the year
Of new beginning

I assumed it meant a year
Of beauty and bliss

But then in remembrance
I realize, the Most High's ways
Are not our ways.
That my suffering is eternal

For new beginning

Doesn't always
Result in new flowers
But in new thorns.

Many countries had new beginnings
That resulted in dictatorships and war
Many people had new beginnings
In COVID, where suffering came anew

So while I shall
Keep Faith in the endurance
Of my challenges
Faith is dimming, on new fruit

I accept that my suffering
Pain, emptiness, brokenness
Shall be springboard fresh
New and worst weeds

In my life, shall arise.

I shall keep Faith
In my ability to endure
21st century, suffering and pain

But nothing more.
I shall keep Faith
In my vigilance
Of incoming despair

For I'm losing
Mere dream of hope
Of even tiny deliverance
Of my eternal pain and suffering

I accept that my suffering is eternal
That my joy's minimal
Even as a small part
Of my Being desires so

It's not my place

To ask for what I wish

I accept my new beginning
The Kingdom of Suffering rises
2024, another year of endurance
Except with more thorns
With little freshwater or wine

I wish you all
A happy blessed
New beginning, full of love
Community and fresh
Garden of life

Suffering is inevitable for all
But I ensure you, light
In the abyss, awaits
New life shall spring

For everything shall come

As for myself, the abyss
Is gazing at me
As for many others
It's the same

My insignificance in the Cosmos
Under the eyes of the Most High
Who's ways are not my ways
Dust I came. Dust I shall return.

A new beginning awaits
For me, to submit fully
Depths of suffering and pain
For I shall endure eternity
My heart hungers for hope
In at least a tiny dandelion
But even my heart
Know what's to come.

My Lord, shall you help me
Reclaim my dying hope.

A new beginning
Of suffering, pain, emptiness
Of endurance, vigilance and Stoicism
Nothing more

I shall endure, or not
In the year 2024
Accept my place in the Cosmos
Accepting beauty in suffering

Even if this new year
Or any year's
I never find
Light in the Abyss.

Dawn of Stillness

Bright sun cloaked
By gray clouds above
Sun's rays dimly seen
At a distance within gray sea

Of the somber atmosphere
Brown, red, and beige leaves
Carried by kinetic winds
Onto destination toward rebirth

Guided with infinite peace
Alongside birds upwards
Moving in union
With currents of air

Door opens, winds blows
Some entering residence
Through door, offering

Tranquility within structure

Upon relinquished amity
Replaced by contented emptiness
A taste of nirvana
For barren edifice of dwellings

Willingly taking the offer
Desiring to embrace hope
Of reconnecting with Being
Internally so as to finally
Rest aching soul of brokenness

Walking out beige house
Tall, workable, plain
Having all capacity to living
Yet lacking essence for life

Closing door behind me
Looking ahead and begins

One's walk toward lake
Release from ambivalent serenity

Hands-on pocket.
Walking straight then right
Towards inner emancipation
As I turn to my right

Walking past suburban houses
Well-built, full of pristine
Ordinary, plain, orderly
Yet dry, perished, crumbling

Even houses full of color
Such as one house painted
In baby and cobalt blue
Cracks, mold, and dust

Molded onto its very identity
As if their youth is eternally tarnished

Only robust design keeps it from crumbing
Under its decay as it accepts its barrenness

Journeying onward straight
Feet stepping on red, orange, green
Leaves, resting on ground as
Those of old gently rest

Nearing the kind lake
Moving gracefully as if
Knowing and accepting itself
Motioning in full calmness with nature

With hard yet smooth pavement
Between lake and tender grass
The hallway between interior chasm
And innermost peace

Words coming in from above
As I continue to walk nearer

You'll never find peace
Yet here I walk

Crossing sterile road
Stepping into desired outcome
That once seemed a fantasy
Only known in fairytales

Voyaging at the pavement
Feet going on grass
Treading onto becoming
Rooted in utmost unification
Of myself

Dirt below my feet
A part of nature
Not an aberration

Continuing on, stopping
At tranquil lake

Looking down, I see
Eyes gazing at familiar face

Gazing at myself
Large deep scars across face
Head to lower lip
Brokenness fabric of existence

Taking a deep breath
From my inner Being
Breathing it out
Into the river

The man-made winds
Blown-in reflection
Cracks from face to neck
Dissipates in smooth succession
Clouds open up, revealing the sun
Ray's shining on reflection

I smile at reflection, for the first time
In many years, he smiles back
Smiling like a new man

Connected to his internal heaven
Peacefulness overwhelms me
Stillness enters my soul like an old friend
Looking closely to see

Small mark remaining
On right side of the head
Memorial of shameful past
Grinning warmly

It's as the dirt of grass
A part of creation
Not an arbitration

Imperfect as it is
Acknowledging it, not in shame

But as the regular part of the process
Of all living things shaping itself

Just as red leaves
Surrounding my feet
Is the coming of green leaves
Not death of new creation

Blue streams appear
Gray clouds dissipate
Steadily as sun appears
Shining brightly in triumph

Staring up
Wind blows past me
Spirit within calm
Feeling internal nourishment

Clouds, leaves, winds
Continue motion yet

Stillness pulses all aspects
Of nature itself

As if in an everlasting motion
Of a relaxing walk
As me and the sun
Share in a calm embrace

Of our Being

Head going toward lake
Soul and body connect
Feet rooted in self
Self-united in nature

For as the winds blow
My essence is calm
As I and nature
Embrace our perpetual

Dawn of Stillness

Milton Keynes UK
Ingram Content Group UK Ltd.
UKHW051202040324
438885UK00014B/753